Sojourn

By United Library

https://campsite.bio/unitedlibrary

Table of Contents

Table of Contents 2

Disclaimer 4

Introduction 5

Sojourner Truth 7

Biography 11

Emancipation (1826-1835) 17

The anti-slavery activist (1835-1843) 27

Sojourner Truth and Millerism (1843-1844) 33

Association for Education and Industry (1844-1846) 36

The revival 40

The American Civil War (1861-1865) 49

Freedmen's Bureau (1864-1868) 55

Privacy policy 64

Written transcriptions by Sojourner Truth 65

Tributes 67

Other books by United Library 70

Disclaimer

This biography book is a work of nonfiction based on the public life of a famous person. The author has used publicly available information to create this work. While the author has thoroughly researched the subject and attempted to depict it accurately, it is not meant to be an exhaustive study of the subject. The views expressed in this book are those of the author alone and do not necessarily reflect those of any organization associated with the subject. This book should not be taken as an endorsement, legal advice, or any other form of professional advice. This book was written for entertainment purposes only.

Introduction

Explore the extraordinary life of Sojourner Truth, an intrepid abolitionist and advocate of civil and women's rights in America. Born into slavery in New York, her journey to freedom in 1826 marked the beginning of her lifelong commitment to fighting injustice. In particular, she became the first black woman to win a case against a white man to get her son back.

In 1843, inspired by a divine calling, she renamed herself Sojourner Truth and embarked on a mission to spread hope and truth in the countryside. Her powerful, impromptu speech to the Ohio Women's Rights Convention in 1851, known as "Am I Not a Woman?", resonated deeply during the Civil War, challenging stereotypes and pleading for equality.

Throughout the war, Truth played a crucial role in recruiting black troops for the Union army. Then she campaigned tirelessly for land grants for formerly enslaved people, symbolized by the promise of "forty acres and a mule". Her legacy as an advocate for women and African-Americans lives on, inspiring generations to fight for justice and equality.

Explore the extraordinary life of Sojourner Truth and be inspired to stand up for what's right!

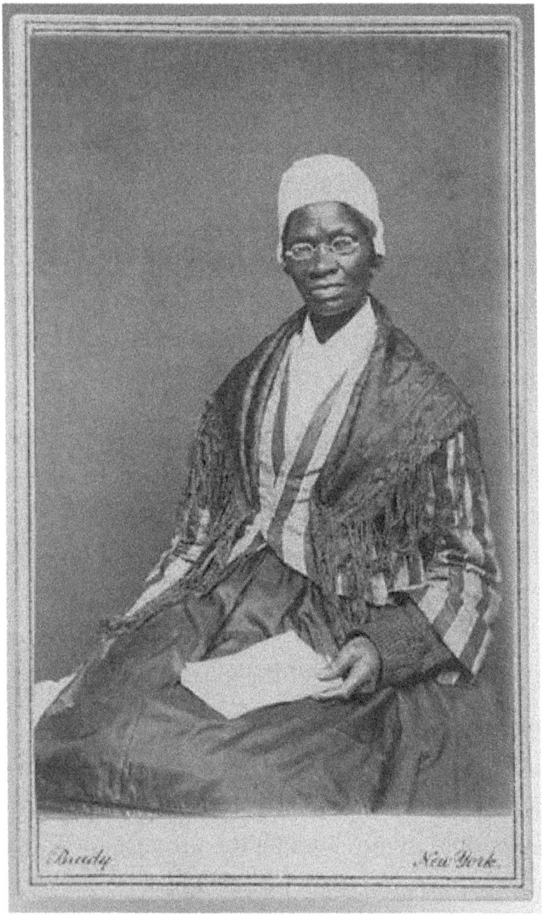
Brady
New York

Sojourner Truth

Sojourner Truth, (birth name Isabella Baumfree, known as Belle, later Isabella Wagenen) born probably in 1797 in Hurley, a town in the former Dutch colony of Ulster County, New York, and died November 26, 1883 in Battle Creek, Michigan, was an evangelical Christian preacher. She was a reformer and one of the most committed African-American abolitionists, as well as a campaigner for voting rights for both black and white women.

Born into slavery to slave parents, she bore the names of her various owners. She bore Isabella Baumfree's name from 1797 to 1827. She was married against her will. Unable to obtain emancipation despite the law of 1826, she ran away and took the name Isabella van Wagenen, in honor of the Quaker couple who took her in.

In 1828, Isabella Wagenen, supported by Quakers, won her case against the slaveholder who abusively held her son. She became the first black woman to win a case against a white man for the freedom of a family member.

While preaching in Manhattan's slums, she meets preachers Elijah Pierson (en) and Robert Matthews (en), a manipulative impostor. This inspired her to affirm her own faith. She attends the anti-slavery Zion African Methodist Episcopal Church, while in New York, violence against African-Americans increases. She befriended African-American activists and joined the *Underground Railroad* to help fugitive slaves. The assassination of Elijah Parish Lovejoy and the Amistad affair decide Isabelle Wagenen to take up the fight against slavery.

On the day of Pentecost in 1843, she chose to take the name Sojourner Truth, following a mystical revelation. Through the power of her preaching, she became a symbol of the ability of the poor, and especially women, to rise up and emancipate themselves, thanks, she believed, to the power of the Holy Spirit.

Sojourner Truth then found in the Northampton Association for Education and Industry a real democratic, fraternal life, without distinction of class or race. She forged lasting friendships with activists like Frederick Douglass, but the community, crippled by debt, had to cease operations.

Sojourner Truth could neither read nor write, so she dictated her autobiography, which was successfully published in 1850 as *Narrative of Sojourner Truth*. She was invited to lecture on women's rights and against the Fugitive Slave Act, along with other African-American activists. Violent controversies erupted between them as to whether or not they were fighting for women's rights and African-American rights at the same time. Truth made a name for herself with her speech *Ain't I a Woman?*

delivered on May 29, 1851 at the 1851 Ohio Women's Congress in Akron.

Sojourner Truth spoke at all anti-slavery and feminist rallies. Although opposed to the Civil War, she supported the Northern troops of the Union Army. With the Progressive Friends (en) of Longwwod, she presented a brief to President Abraham Lincoln on the emancipation of slaves. This was her first meeting with the President. She sees him again during his re-election campaign in 1864.

After the Civil War, Sojourner Truth and her friends became involved in the defense of freedmen through the Bureau of Refugees, Freedmen and Abandoned Lands. In 1867, Sojourner Truth addressed the convention of the American Equal Rights Association and drew attention to the plight of recently freed women of color, reiterating the link between white and black women's rights. Noting the state of exclusion and poverty of the freedwomen, Sojourner Truth fought for a settlement project in the territories available in the American West. Despite her efforts and a tour of several months in Kansas and with members of Congress and the Senate, she had to abandon the project, which was neither voted nor financed.

At the end of 1874, Sojourner Truth fell ill, but she resumed her lecture series from 1878 to 1880. Some of her lectures were covered by the press. She died of exhaustion at her last home, Battle Creek, on November 26, 1883.

Along with Harriet Tubman, Sojourner Truth is one of the most famous African-American women of the 19th century.

Biography

The early years 1797- 1826

Isabella Baumfree was born around 1797 in Hurley, a town in the former Dutch colony of Ulster County, New York. Her parents were Makewe, renamed James Bomefree, also known as Baumfree, which in Dutch means "tree", and Elizabeth, nicknamed Betsey or "Mau-Mau Bett". Both are said to have originated in present-day Ghana. They gave birth to Isabella Baumfree around 1797 (the year 1797 is supported by the testimony of her first masters). She was the second-to-last of their twelve or thirteen children. They were slaves of Colonel Johannes Hardenberg, who addressed them only in Dutch so that they could not communicate with their predominantly English-speaking entourage. The young Isabella Baumfree, nicknamed "Belle", spoke only Dutch, a language she retained throughout her life.

The Hardenberg family was a pillar of the Dutch Calvinist community, the Dutch Reformed Church, based in the county of Ulster. They then embraced the pietism of theologian Theodorus Jacobus Frelinghuysen (en), whose teachings they passed on to their slaves, notably Elizabeth Beaumfree, who in turn passed them on to her daughter Isabella, who was to be permanently influenced by them.

Johannes Hardenberg died in 1799. The Beaumfree family was part of the inheritance passed on to his son Charles Hardenberg, who took her and a dozen other slaves to their new home in the nearby hills. With him, the slaves' living conditions deteriorated, their new dwellings were insanitary, and Isabella's parents were exhausted, worn out both by working in the fields and by their cold, damp dwelling during the winters. Despite the harsh living conditions, the Beaumfree family passed on a moral education to their children.

In May 1808, Charles Hardenberg died, and his heirs decided to auction off his cattle, horses and slaves, including the Beaumfree family. But the heirs decide to keep the Baumfree parents, even to set them free; once free, Isabella's parents continue to work for the Hardenbergs. For her part, Isabella Baumfree is auctioned off with a consignment of sheep for the sum of $100, and becomes the property of a merchant, John Nealy, who lives in the village of Twaalfskill, near Kingston in the county of Ulster. He is brutal towards her. Isabella Baumfree's poor English made her make mistakes when carrying out orders, so John Nealy and his wife regularly whipped her - John Nealy went so far as to beat her with a poker. Isabella Baumfree tries to learn English from her masters, but they don't have the patience. As Mr Nealy continues to yell at her, she gradually learns English, but retains her Dutch accents. In this atmosphere of abuse, separated from her parents, her only refuge is prayer and trust in God.

One winter evening, freedman James Baumfree visits his daughter Isabella. He discovers that she's not wearing winter clothes, and notices the scars from the beatings on his daughter's back. Enraged, James Baumfree promises to find a solution. In 1810, he convinced Martinus Schryver, a fisherman and innkeeper of Dutch descent, to buy his daughter. Schryver needed a servant. The Nealy family got rid of Isabella Baumfree, selling her for $175 to Martinus Schryver. He offered her a more comfortable life, with warm winter clothes and good food. She no longer works in the fields, but is assigned to domestic chores and service at the inn, where she discovers a world of drinkers with a mug in their hand, thinking only of dancing or gambling, a world of vulgarity. Several customers try to seduce her, but to no avail; she remains chaste. During this period, she learns of her mother's disappearance. Then Martinus Schryver defaults on his payments and sells Isabella to John J. Dumont, a Huguenot descendant and wealthy landowner from New Paltz, still in Ulster County.

The years at New Paltz

John J. Dumont assigns Isabella Baumfree, like his ten other slaves, to the domestic life of his home; she is assigned to the kitchen, where she excels, and at the same time gradually improves her English. While John J. Dumont was tolerant and patient with her, his wife was not, and regularly reprimanded her. The tensions between Isabella Baumfree and her masters are probably due to jealousy among the servants. Kate, in particular, a white servant, blames Isabella Baumfree for her mistakes and sabotages her work, notably by polluting the water in the pot in which she boils the potatoes. Gertrude Dumont, nicknamed Gerty, the Dumont couple's daughter, takes a liking to Isabella Baumfreee and puts her in the clear by exposing Kate's maneuvers to discredit her.

During this period, Isabella Baumfree received basic religious training from the Dumont family clerk and John J. Dumont's coachman, Cato, who acted as preacher to the slaves.

In 1815, at the Pinkster (en) feast celebrated on Pentecost by the African-American slaves of Dutch Reformed Church owners. Isabella Baumfree is 18. She falls in love with Robert, a slave owned by a master named Catlin. Catlin objected to Robert and Isabella's relationship and imposed a companion on Robert, a slave with whom he could sire new slaves of his own. Despite the ban, Robert and Isabella continue to see each other in secret. Catlin, who suspects this, sets a trap and beats Robert with a stick in front of Isabella Baumfree. When the beating takes place at John J. Dumont's house, Dumont, alerted by Baumfree's cries, intervenes to stop Catlin and his son from beating him. To ensure that Robert is not beaten to death, he accompanies the Catlins, with Robert in chains, back to their home.

This incident reminds his master John J. Dumont that Isabella Baumfree is of childbearing age and that it's time to look for a man to unite her with. He chooses one of his slaves, a man named Thomas, who has already fathered two sons, sold to other owners. Neither Thomas nor Baumfree have any feelings for each other, but that's none of their owner's business. That said, Isabella Baumfree manages to obtain a marriage ceremony from her master, which is performed by an African-American cleric. Despite the arbitrary nature of their union, the couple learn to respect and appreciate each other. Their union produced five children, four daughters and one son: Diana, Elisabeth, Sophia and Peter, one of whom died prematurely without a first name. Two of their daughters were sold.

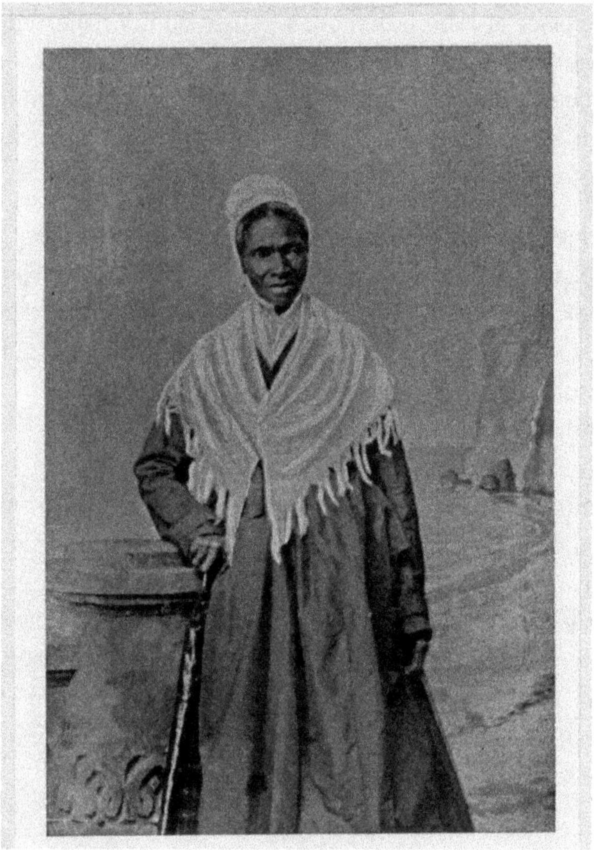

Emancipation (1826-1835)

New York State and the abolition of slavery

After the Revolutionary War, the *Quakers* (Religious Society of Friends) were the first to campaign in an organized way against slavery and to question the right of one person to own another as a slave. Under the impetus of Antoine Bénézet and John Woolman, anti-slavery organizations were created. The first American anti-slavery society, the *Pennsylvania Abolition Society, was* founded in Philadelphia on April 14, 1775. This first society was emulated in every state from Massachusetts to Virginia, as was the *New York Manumission Society* founded in 1785.

In 1817, under pressure from the Quakers and the *New York Manumission Society*, the State of New York passed a first law stating that slaves born after July 4, 1799 would be progressively emancipated: women at age 25 and men at age 28. Then an amendment specified that on July 4, 1827, all slaves born before 1799 would be emancipated. This law meant that Isabella Baumfree, aged 29, could apply for emancipation from July 4, 1826.

Emancipation denied

When, on July 4, 1826, Isabella Baumfree asked John J. Dumont to emancipate her, he refused, believing that he had not gotten his money's worth. Baumfree knows that pressure from the owners is strong. There are cases of slaves being murdered because of their demands to be free. Her only solution is to flee. She and her daughter Sophia take refuge with neighbors Isaac and Maria van Wagenen, who live in Wagondale, Ulster.

The Wagenen years (1826-1828)

Isabella takes the Wagenen name, becoming Isabella Wagenen. Her sensibility brings her closer to what today is known as Pentecostalism, inspiration by the Holy Spirit, which she also calls The Spirit, a movement also known as *Christian Perfection*. Pentecostalism derives from the Pinkster (en) festival, celebrated in particular by African-American slaves owned by members of the Dutch Reformed Church, which is an occasion for singing, dancing and trances that, according to novelist James Fenimore Cooper, resemble saturnalia for blacks.

These feasts commemorate the liberation of the Hebrews, with whom Isabella Wagenen identifies, revealing to her "the glory of God". This revelation would have taken place in the winter of 1827, or more likely after the Pinkster feast celebrated on Pentecost 1827.

Isabella Wagenen, like many former slaves, has only a vague notion of the Creed. What she knows of Christianity can be summed up in the Ten Commandments and stories about the life, death and resurrection of Christ. On the other hand, she proclaims her closeness, even intimacy, with both God and Jesus Christ, whom she considers a friend. She is convinced that she has a special relationship with him, that her visions prepare her to receive the "redemption of Christ".

Also in 1827, while Isabella Wagenen was working in Kingston, she was walking through the city when she heard singing from a Methodist meeting. Approaching the meeting, she was invited to attend. Isabella was impressed by the warmth and welcome of these Christians, and so attended the Saint James Methodist Episcopal Church in Kingston. Here, for the first time in her life, she developed genuinely positive relationships with white women, who encouraged her to train. Isabella Wagenen took courses in Bible studies, discovering Methodist doctrine and the Trinity. She understands that Jesus is a divine being, which strengthens her confidence in him.

Victory in the trial against a slave trader (1828)

Her son Peter had been sold illegally to an Alabama planter. In 1828, Isabella Wagenen, with the help of Quackers friends, sued the slaveholder who held him:

People v. Solomon Gedney. In winning custody of her son, she became the first black woman to win a case against a white man for the freedom of a family member.

The New York years (1828-1835)

Isabella Wagenen attended the John Street Methodist Church (en) in Manhattan, where she made friends with a schoolteacher, Miss Geer, who confirmed that New York offered job opportunities for African-Americans, especially for her son Peter. In September 1828, Isabella Wagenen left the Wagenens to travel to New York with her two children, accompanied by the Grear couple, all devotees of the *Christian Perfection movement*. She earned her living as a domestic servant.

To protect herself from a New York environment unfriendly to African-Americans, she preciously carries a bill certifying her conversion to Methodism, although the precise circumstances of this conversion are unknown.

When Isabella Wagenen learned that John Street services were to become segregated, some for whites, others for African-Americans, she joined a parish of the African Methodist Episcopal (or AME) Church, the Harlem-based congregation headquartered at Mother African Methodist Episcopal Zion Church (en).

New York, like other American cities, was swept by a current of "moral reform" condemning alcohol consumption, gambling and prostitution, which led to poverty and disease. Calls for reform were made to women as guardians of family and religious values.

Elijah Pierson, the street preacher

In 1829 or 1830, Miss Geer invited Isabella Wagenen to Manhattan's Five Points district, known for its slums, shantytowns and high crime rate, so she could preach God's love. Wagenen realized that the neighborhood's inhabitants were especially in need of food, clothing and healthy housing. It was during these visits that she heard about the *Magdalen Asylum*, a shelter for homeless women and prostitutes founded by preacher Elijah Pierson (en) known as the Tishbite (en). This former Presbyterian turned street preacher created a movement strictly attached to the Five Points of Calvinism, derived from the *Christian Perfection* of the austere *Retrenchment Society* and close to millenarianism and Mormonism. Like the prophet Elijah ("Elijah"), Elijah Pierson claimed to have received divine revelation. God is said to have given him the gift of curing illness and the fear of death. As a reminder of this revelation, he takes the name *Tishbite, which is* the Old Testament qualification for the prophet Elijah. Elijah Pierson and his wife Sarah Stanford Pierson preach particularly to call prostitutes to conversion. It was in the name of his faith that Elijah Pierson built the *Magdalen Asylum* in the Bowery district. Despite sectarianism among Elijah Pierson's followers, Isabella Wagenen reveres his radical perfectionism and turns away from Methodism to join him. She is housed in the *Magdalen Asylum*. Like the Piersons, Isabella Wagenen also preaches to prostitutes on the streets, and regularly prays with the Piersons in their home.

Robert Matthews aka Matthias

In May 1832, Isabella Wagenen and the Piersons were visited by Robert Matthews (en), who called himself Matthias ("Matthew") as Christ's last and twelfth apostle and evangelist. He presents himself as "God the Father with power over all things". Robert Matthews, born in 1788, is a businessman who, after being raised Presbyterian, joined the United Church of Zion (en), also known as the *River Brethren*, which is a synthesis of Pietism and Anabaptist Mennonism. Robert Matthews, claims he has been given the mission to reveal true Christianity and the coming of God's kingdom on earth, as well as the damnation of Christians who condemn the *Christian Perfection* movement. He also preaches reincarnation for followers of the true religion. Thanks to his Jewish grandmother, he claims to have inherited the gift of prophecy. Margaret, his wife, believes his ideas come from Mordecai Manuel Noah, but his conceptions of the Temple of God and the holy celestial city, the New Jerusalem, come from the Book of Revelation. Like one of his teachers, the Presbyterian perfectionist Edward Norris Kirk (en), Robert Matthews is an abolitionist. He began preaching in the streets of Albany, then disappeared, only to reappear in New York. Although Elijah Pierson initially suspected Robert Matthews of being an impostor, he was seduced by him and persuaded to combine their messages. Elijah Pierson became Robert Matthews' John the Baptist, announcing the coming of the kingdom of God, renamed the Kingdom of Matthew. Despite Robert Matthews' inherited High Church views of women as devils, witches and seducers, Isabella Wagenen is impressed by his personality. With only the vaguest notions of Christianity, she is easily subjugated by him, kneeling before him and kissing his feet. She worked for him for several years. She stayed as a maid in Robert Matthews' headquarters, nicknamed "*The Zion Hill*", located on a farm near Sing Sing belonging to Benjamin and Ann Folger. Isabella Wagenen took part in all the religious ceremonies organized by Robert Matthews.

The impostor unmasked

It is becoming increasingly well known that Robert Matthews uses his followers' money to live the high life. He is also suspected of suffering from bipolar disorder, accompanied by violence. A family of his followers reports his behavior to the police, who go to his home to arrest him. Isabella Wagenen, naive and loyal, tries to protect him, but to no avail. Robert Matthews is committed to the psychiatric ward of Bellevue Hospital. Elijah Pierson and Isabella Wagenen succeed in having him released. However, they begin to distrust Robert Matthews and distance themselves from him. Isabella Wagenen leaves Robert Matthews' headquarters and moves back to New York, where Miss Geer finds her a job as a maid.

A scandalous trial

Elijah Pierson, who remained at *Zion Hill*, suffered several ailments that became increasingly worrying from the summer of 1834 onwards. He regularly suffered bouts of fever and was bedridden for days at a time. Robert Matthews and his followers refused to call in a doctor, believing Elijah Pierson's ailments to be the work of the devil. Then, suddenly, on August 4 1834, Elijah Pierson died. Investigations point to murky circumstances, against a backdrop of financial disputes with Robert Matthews, claims by Benjamin and Ann Folger to take over from Elijah Pierson, and allegations of sexual relations. Benjamin and Ann Folger accuse Robert Matthews and Isabella Wagenen of murdering Elijah Pierson by poisoning. They were imprisoned, and at the trial, which began on April 18, 1835, Isabella Wagenen was acquitted, as the court found no evidence of poisoning.

Assertiveness

Isabella Wagenen realizes that she has been manipulated by both Elijah Pierson and Robert Matthews with their false promises of a loving community of believers. She decides to reject any exegesis of the Bible other than her own, and to take a critical look at those who claim to be Christians. Disappointment and a critical eye will enable Isabella Wagenen to assert herself.

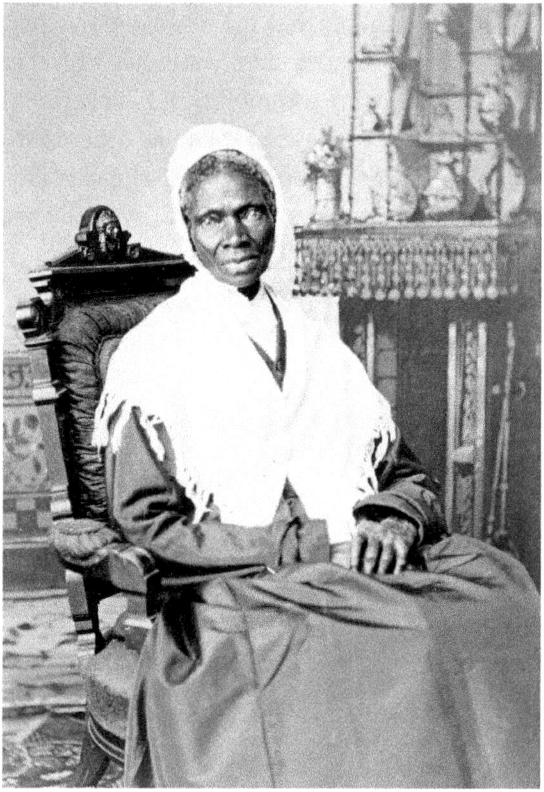

The anti-slavery activist (1835-1843)

New York racists

African-Americans are regularly insulted and beaten by people who do not accept New York's emancipation laws. Public services shun African-Americans just as public schools turn away their children. African-American notables such as Samuel Cornish, Thomas Van Renssalaer, James McCune Smith (en), Charles Bennett Ray (en) report the discrimination they suffer at the hands of their white colleagues, who refuse their admission to clubs and associations.

Sion African Methodist Episcopal Church

Isabella Wagenen initially withdrew from any political or social involvement. She settled in New York with her two children, earning a living as a cook, maid and washerwoman. She also assiduously attended services at the Zion African Methodist Episcopal Church in Harlem.

This church is led by Bishop Christopher Rush (Bishop) (en), who holds resolutely anti-slavery sermons. He is also president of the Phoenix Society (New York) (en), an anti-slavery society bringing together whites and African-Americans. This is also where Isabella Wagenen hears of African-American publisher David Ruggles (en), who has formed an African-American vigilante militia, headquartered at the Zion African Methodist Episcopal Church in Harlem.

Female preachers in the face of machismo

At Zion Church, Isabella Wagenen befriended African-American activists like Eliza Day and Hester Lane (en), who combined religious faith with social protest. With them and others, Wagenen joined the *Underground Railroad* to help fugitive slaves. Their actions are contested by men steeped in macho prejudice. *The Colored American* magazine castigated these women, asking their husbands, partners and parents to keep them at home and give them domestic tasks. Many preachers, such as Jarena Lee, Zilpha Elaw (en), Rebecca Cox Jackson (en), Julia A. J. Foote (en) are shunned by men in the name of prevailing Victorian morality. Only William Lloyd Garrison ignores these prejudices by opening the columns of his newspaper *The Liberator* to women. In January 1831, African-American Maria W. Stewart (en) inaugurated The *Liberator*'s "Ladies department" column. Her fiery articles on African-American emancipation, inspired by her friend David Walker, foreshadowed the preaching of Isabella Wagenen.

The influence of Maria W. Stewart

Maria W. Stewart published her first essay, *Religion and the Pure Principles of Morality,* in 1831, which led her to lecture to all-African-American women's clubs, first in Boston in April 1832. She addressed men in September 1832, then left Boston for New York, where she held her first lecture on September 21, 1833. She became vice-principal of a school in 1837. Maria W. Stewart attends St. Philip's Episcopal Church (Manhattan). Maria W. Stewart's various lectures were copied and read by anti-slavery societies and churches, especially African-American ones. This is how Isabella Wagenen discovered Maria W. Stewart's ideas on women's rights and the possibility of being a preacher like Julia Pell.

American women against slavery

Wagenen is attentive to the rise of slavery abolition among American women, both white and black. The most powerful mixed-gender women's organizations are the Philadelphia Female Anti-Slavery Society (en), whose members include the wives of James Forten and Robert Purvis - an association also considered the cradle of American feminism - and the Boston Female Anti-Slavery Society (en), whose members include sisters Lucy M. Ball and Martha Violet Ball (en), the Weston sisters... Among the Whites are Lucretia Mott and Abby Kelley, who would later join Isabella Wagenen.

In 1837, a women's convention was held in a small church on New York's Houston Street. It was the first inter-racial convention to feature ten African-American women, some of whom were Wagenen acquaintances. Among them were Maria W. Stewart, Hester Lane (en) and the wives of James Forten and Robert Purvis, who presented their experiences of racism. Angelina Emily Grimké reads her pamphlet *An Appeal to the Women of the Nominally Free States,* a manifesto calling for measures to end slavery and racism. The appeal incorporates the poem *We are thy sisters,* written by Sarah Louisa Forten Purvis for the occasion.

Isabella Wagenen's fight against slavery

The first decisive event was the assassination of Elijah Parish Lovejoy on November 7, 1837, in Alton, Illinois. The crime was committed by a mob of racist slavers who couldn't stand his condemnations of lynching, his creation of an Illinois chapter of the American Anti-Slavery Society and his anti-slavery newspaper *The Saint Louis Observer*.

In 1839, Lewis Tappan (en) organized a meeting at the Broadway United Church of Christ (en) under the auspices of the American Anti-Slavery Society (AASS), attended by five thousand abolitionists. At this meeting, William Lloyd Garrison and David Ruggles succeed in passing a resolution for the full participation of women on an equal footing with men. This resolution was one of the reasons for a secession within the AASS, and Lewis Tappan founded the American and Foreign Anti-Slavery Society (en). Isabella Wagenen was far removed from these debates, but William Lloyd Garrison and David Ruggles' resolution paved the way.

The second decisive event was the Amistad affair, which mobilized abolitionists in the same way as the murder of Elijah Parish Lovejoy, and confirmed Isabella Wagenen's commitment to the anti-slavery cause. Joseph Cinqué, who led the Amistad revolt, inspired the emergence of new leaders in the African-American community, such as Charles Lenox Remond (en), Frederick Douglass and Henry Highland Garnet. Isabella Wagenen, who attended the Broadway United Church of Christ, heard Joseph Cinqué recount his heroic mutiny in November 1841. She sees it as a message from God to mobilize her forces.

Isabella Wagenen becomes Sojourner Truth

All these events left their mark on Isabella Wagenen, and in 1843 she decided to take the name Sojourner Truth, the one who "sojourns for truth and justice", and is driven by the spirit of resistance.

The exact circumstances of this name change are unclear. It seems that on June 1, 1843, the day of Pentecost, she took part in a prayer meeting. As she left it, walking towards Long Island, she received a call from the Holy

Spirit to leave her ordinary life and embrace a life of service to a divine mission. Her new name would be a celebration of her emancipation from the "house of bondage" similar to that of the Hebrews freed by God from Egyptian bondage, as well as a condemnation of the cities of bondage, which like Sodom would be annihilated by God. His mission is to proclaim God as the liberator of the oppressed.

Her revelation was followed by an adherence to the Millerism founded by William Miller, a Baptist pastor, who announced the second return of Christ for the year 1844. Sojourner Truth followed in the footsteps of other itinerant preachers, such as the African-American Zilpha Elaw and Harriet Livermore (en), who were convinced that they were living in the last days of humanity. Other figures such as Angelina Emily Grimké and Theodore Weld also share this opinion. Abolitionist Gerrit Smith, who also subscribes to the end-of-the-world thesis, welcomes Sojourner Truth and Harriet Tubman to his home.

Sojourner Truth and Millerism (1843-1844)

Sojourner Truth and William Miller

The links between Isabella Wagenen's choice to adopt the name Sojourner Truth and Millerism are necessary to understand her journey. William Miller, born in 1782, was a farmer in Washington County, New York. Robert Matthews was also born in this county. According to biographer Nell Irvin Painter, they apparently knew each other and were both inspired by the dispensationalism spread in the United States by John Nelson Darby. This theology, based on the reading of the Book of Daniel, establishes the great periods of Salvation and the date of the end of time - or Judgment Day - when those who have sinned will be condemned to burn in hell. Dispensationalists' mission is to call as many sinners as possible to repentance and salvation.

William Miller, before joining dispensationalism, was an abolitionist Baptist minister. As early as 1831, he began holding conferences in which he prophesied the coming of Christ to condemn sinners and glorify the saints. In January 1843, he predicted that Christ would return between March 21, 1843 and March 21, 1844. The June 8,

1843 issue of *The Midnight Cry,* edited by William Miller, publishes an article by Joshua V. Himes (en), who states that according to the Book of Daniel, the end times era will begin in the year 1843. The warning signs are that the population is living in an "age of debauchery".

Sojourner Truth, who listens to the William Miller lectures, is cautious. She rejects his predictions. For her, the coming of Christ is conditional on an era of perfection, even though she says "*the* Lord is as near as he can be". She prefers a spiritual presence to a physical one. Her wisdom inspires the Windsor Locks community of Adventists.

Winter of 1844

Sojourner Truth is looking for a place to spend the approaching winter of 1844. At first, she is tempted to join the Fruitlands (Transcendentalism) (en) community, founded by Amos Bronson Alcott, where she might find new insights into philosophy and spirituality. On the advice of friends, she turned to a Shaker community founded by Mother Ann Lee and located in Enfield, Connecticut. But their ecstatic practices and contempt for society aroused Sojourner Truth's distrust. Finally, she chose to spend the winter of 1844 in a cooperative community in Northampton, Massachusetts.

A landmark sermon by Sojourner Truth

Sojourner Truth's skeptical caution increased when the year 1844 ended without the fulfillment of William Miller's prophesied advent of Christ. The Millerist community was stunned. Sojourner Truth is invited to speak in various cities. After Hartford and Cabotville, she held a sermon in Springfield, Massachusetts, before a congregation of bewildered pastors. She explains why God's people need not be afraid. She draws on the Book of Daniel to explain that God's children need not fear living in the midst of the corrupt world symbolized by Babylon. The pastors present are amazed that an illiterate African-American woman is able to use their biblical hermeneutics to refute their teaching. With this sermon, she becomes a prominent figure to whom they can relate.

Association for Education and Industry (1844-1846)

A Fourierist community

The Northampton Association for Education and Industry, now known as the Ross Farm (Northampton, Massachusetts) (en), is one of 270 Fourierist-inspired communities in the United States. It was founded in 1842 by radical abolitionists and led by George Benson (Quaker) (en), William Lloyd Garrison's brother-in-law. Since its foundation, a number of prominent abolitionists have lectured there, including Frederick Douglass, Theodore Weld, Henry Clarke Wright (en), Lucy Stone, Charles Burleigh (en), George Thomson, Charles Lenox Remond (en), Wendell Philips, Sylvester Graham.

An involved community

When Sojourner Truth joined the community, it included 210 members from eight states, most notably Massachusetts and Connecticut. Frederick Douglass notes that there is a real democratic, fraternal life, without distinction of class or race. Sojourner Truth is assigned to the laundry. Here she met feminist abolitionists such as Methodist minister Giles Stebbins, James Boyle, David Ruggles, Lydia Maria Child and her husband, journalist David Lee Child (en). It was in this community that she first met Frederick Douglass, who had come to see his friend David Ruggles. She also struck up a friendship with self-emancipated slave Basil Dorsey (en). She also became involved in the Underground Railroad network, the community being a refuge-stop for African-American slaves fleeing to freedom. She provides them with shelter, food, clothing and comfort.

Decisive friendships

Sojourner Truth forges lasting friendships with Frederick Douglass, the clergyman, abolitionist and women's rights advocate, Parker Pillsbury (en) and Stephen Symonds Foster (en), a radical abolitionist married to Abby Kelley Foster, who will be fellow travelers.

Sojourner Truth pacifies a conflict

At a community meeting, hooligans disrupt the assembly by whistling and booing. The organizers try in vain to calm them down. The gang of thugs, armed with bats and sticks, get excited and threaten to set the place on fire. Fear grips the crowd. Sojourner Truth, after an initial movement of fear, confronts the troublemakers. She climbs onto a platform and begins to sing in a loud voice a hymn glorifying the resurrection of Christ. Hearing her, the thugs are stopped in their tracks, ask Sojourner Truth to continue singing and show her religious respect. She understands that behind all this heckling and anti-social behavior, these young people need recognition, validation. She begins a dialogue with them, answering their every question, demonstrating her ability to break down the barriers between people.

The end of the community and the publication of *Narrative of Sojourner Truth*

The community, experiencing great financial difficulties, was forced to cease its activities on November 1, 1846. This was a great disappointment for Sojourner Truth, who had found a place where she could freely express herself and be respected. In memory of this "good time", George Benson welcomed Sojourner Truth and her daughter Sophia into his family home, where she worked as a governess. In April 1850, Samuel Hill, one of the community's founders, sells her a parcel of community land for $300 to pay off debts. Some people, probably Sarah Benson or Dolly Stetson, introduced her to Gilbert Olive. He offered to write her biography, following the example of Frederick Douglass's autobiography *A Narrative of the Life of Frederick Douglass, an American Slave, which was* a success from the start. Sojourner Truth agrees. Gilbert Olive's interviews with her were compiled and published in 1850 under the title *Narrative of Sojourner Truth*. William Lloyd Garrison arranged for publication through the printer of his newspaper, *The Liberator*, George Brown Yerrinton, who also edited *Narrative of the Life of Frederick Douglass, an American Slave*. With the profits from the book's sales, Sojourner Truth is able to pay for the construction of his house.

The revival

Evangelism and women's rights

In 1849, Sojourner Truth was invited to speak at a convention of the American Anti-Slavery Society in New York. She recalls the trials she has had to endure since her emancipation, how faith saved her, gave her self-confidence and shaped her evangelical vision.

Sojourner Truth added to her evangelical preaching the demand for women's rights, which she regularly reiterated at meetings such as those of the American Anti-Slavery Society. At other meetings, such as that of 1850, she makes the same speech at a women's rights meeting held in Worcester, Massachusetts - a meeting that follows in the footsteps of the 1848 Seneca Falls Convention organized by Elizabeth Cady Stanton, Lucretia Mott and others. Also present was Amy Post (en), who became a fellow traveler with Sojourner Truth.

The Fugitive Slave Law of 1850

To stem the exodus of fugitive slaves aided by Northerners, the predominantly Democratic Congress passed the Fugitive Slave Act in 1850. Among other things, it made any police officer liable to a fine of up to $1,000 for refusing to arrest a suspected runaway slave. It obliges all law enforcement officials to arrest anyone suspected of being a runaway slave, without the owner having to prove possession. Suspects can no longer even go to court to defend themselves. Finally, anyone helping a fugitive by providing care or even food is liable to six months' imprisonment and a fine of up to $1,000.

This law aroused anger and protests of all kinds, and encouraged the emergence of new figures, notably among African-American women such as Mary Ann Shadd Cary, Harriet Tubman, Frances Ellen Watkins and Sojourner Truth.

Truth claims that this iniquitous law raises a moral protest, that it is contrary to the good of humanity and the spirit of the Constitution. She reiterated her convictions in December 1850 at a meeting in Plymouth, Massachusetts, also attended by Frederick Douglass, George Thompson, William Lloyd Garrison, Charles Burleigh (en). At the meeting, which celebrated the bicentenary of the arrival of the Pilgrim Fathers, everyone made it clear that the Fugitive Act was contrary to the spirit of the Pilgrims and to divine law. Frederick Douglass was pessimistic, fearing that only a war would put an end to the controversy.

The 1851 Ohio Women's Convention in Akron

Sojourner Truth leaves Massachusetts to intervene in the state of Ohio, where many fugitive slaves settled and which is famous for Oberlin College, the first university to admit African-American students. Salem was the site of one of the first women's rights conventions, held in 1850. Violent controversies arose over the rights of women and African-Americans. Frances Dana Barker Gage called for complete equality with men, while Jane Grey Swisshelm demanded recognition of women's rights based on their differences from men. She contrasts their brutal strength with women's elegance, delicacy and finesse. Similarly, on the issue of slavery, Frances Dana Barker Gage links the emancipation of slaves to that of women. Jane Grey Swisshelm, though an abolitionist, was opposed, believing that the two issues should be dealt with separately. The controversies between these two women are published in the *Saturday Visitor* newspaper. Jane Grey Swisshelm criticizes the presence of Frederick Douglass and Sojourner Truth at a meeting on women's rights held in Worcester in 1850 - their interventions having introduced the question of skin color into the debate. For Jane Grey Swisshelm, African-American women had to stand up for themselves as women, regardless of the color of their skin. Her conservative stance was strongly contested even by feminists. Pastor Parker Pillsbury (en) reminds Jane Grey Swisshelm, in the columns of the *Saturday Visitor*, that the question of race and that of women's rights cannot be ignored in terms of what they have in common.

It was in this tense climate that Sojourner Truth, supported by Pastor Marius Robinson (en), invited herself to speak at the Ohio Women's Rights Convention held at the Akron Unitarian Church on May 28 and 29, 1851. The meeting was organized by Frances Dana Barker Gage and Hannah Tracy Cutler (en). The latter wondered who this African-American woman was who wanted to speak - which was unusual - so they invited her for an interview. Sojourner Truth presented them with her biography, written by George Benson *Narrative, and* each bought a copy. However, both Frances Dana Barker Gage and Hannah Tracy Cutler tell her that no one knows her, and are skeptical about how she will be received.

The famous speech *Ain't I a Woman?*

When Sojourner Truth delivers her speech at the Akron Convention *Ain't I a Woman?* she speaks of her experience as a slave, but above all of her struggle as a woman; she castigates stereotypes about the "weaker sex" based on an alleged superiority of men; she asserts that women are capable of doing everything men do and more; she refutes clerics who use the Bible to justify women's subordination to men.

There are several versions of this text, perhaps titled *Ain't I a Woman?* because of the repetition of this phrase in her speech. It was a landmark success and the subject of several positive articles, in the Ohio newspaper *The Anti-Slavery Bugle (en)* and others, written by Frances Dana Barker Gage, Elizabeth Cady Stanton, Susan B. Antony, Matilda Joslyn Gage. In 1863, Harriet Beecher Stowe wrote an article for the *Atlantic Monthly* entitled *Sojourner Truth, the Lybian Sybil*.

Opposition on the rise

The 1850s saw the growth of opposition between the abolitionist Northern states and the slaveholding Southern states. The Fugitive Slave Act of 1850 governed the extradition of escaped slaves and their return to their owners. In the same year, the Compromise of 1850, drafted by Senators Henry Clay and Daniel Webster, defined: the entry of new states into the Union (such as California); the delimitation of the border between Texas and the Territory of New Mexico; the reinforcement of the Fugitive Slave Act of 1850; the prohibition of the slave trade in the District of Columbia; and the establishment of a government for the Territory of Utah. The territories of New Mexico and Utah would be able to decide at the time of their admission whether to maintain or abolish slavery. The novelty, which provokes debate, is that from now on the new territories and states will decide for themselves whether or not to allow slavery, which is contrary to the Missouri Compromise of 1820. This was contrary to the Missouri Compromise of 1820, which drew the boundary between slave-owning and abolitionist states along the 36° 30' parallel: north of this line the states were abolitionist, south of it they were slave-owning. The Compromise also facilitated the restitution of slaves who had taken refuge in the northern states, even if they had been emancipated.

Far from calming tensions, the Compromise of 1850 aroused the anger of Northern abolitionists and African-Americans, who organized to fight back against what they considered an iniquitous act. In Boston, New York, Philadelphia and Pittsburgh, abolitionist figures such as Samuel Ringgold Ward (en), Robert Purvis, Martin Delany and Frederick Douglass mobilized public opinion. It was in this climate that Sojourner Truth took the floor, either alongside Frederick Douglass or in his own name at the *New England Anti-Slavery Society* convention.

The African-American flight

Many fugitive slaves, such as Harriet Tubman, no longer felt safe and fled the United States, seeking refuge in Canada. Martin Delany asserts that African-Americans have nothing to expect from the United States, and that their only hope is to migrate to other countries. In 1854, he organized and presided over the first national emigration convention in Cleveland. Sojourner Truth was alarmed by this rise in exasperation, fearing revenge movements by African-Americans against whites without distinction. On September 8, 1853, a convention on women's rights was held in New York, at which she took the floor to say how much she felt like a New Yorker and described herself as a citizen of New York. And despite the Supreme Court's Scott v. Sandford decision of 1857, which ruled that any American of African descent, whether slave or free, could not be an American citizen, she maintained her position. She compares the Supreme Court in Congress to the Persian king Ahasuerus of the Old Testament, fought by Esther. Sojourner Truth speaks of Esther both as a woman and as a Jew belonging to an oppressed people. His metaphor does not go unnoticed. Many Americans know the Bible by heart, including Abraham Lincoln and William Lloyd Garrison. She compares the compassion of King Ahasuerus towards Esther and the Jewish people with the dryness of heart of Congress and the Supreme Court. She repeats that she has no desire to see the enemies of Jews, women or African-Americans killed, but that her mistreated and humiliated people demand respect, not revenge. Unlike Frederick Douglass, who believed slavery would end in bloodshed, Sojourner Truth believed it would end in non-violence.

The crisis

While Sojourner Truth was tirelessly speaking at anti-slavery and feminist meetings, the publication of *Uncle Tom's Cabin* by Harriet Beecher Stowe in 1852 inflamed abolitionist opinion. As soon as it was published, Sojourner Truth had it read. Sojourner Truth and Harriet Beecher Stowe are present, side by side, at several meetings. The black question becomes predominant.

Abolitionist opinion was also inflamed by the hanging of John Brown, who became an anti-slavery hero, as evidenced by, among other things, a meeting held in Boston in 1860 celebrating John Brown's memory.

After Abraham Lincoln's victory in the U.S. presidential election of 1860, the abolitionists grew stronger. Sojourner Truth, who had publicly supported Abraham Lincoln, joined Laura Smith Haviland (en), Josephine Sophia White Griffing (en), Frances Titus (en) Parker Pillsbury, Giles Badger Stebbins and other abolitionist figures to hold a meeting organized by the Michigan Anti-Slavery Society (en). The purpose of the meeting was to put pressure on Lincoln's Republican platform to denounce slavery and various laws such as the Fugitive Slave Act. Abolitionists sought a radical break with the policies of President James Buchanan, who had defended the slaveholding policies of the Southern states. However, since the secession of South Carolina, Lincoln's government was unable to adopt an openly anti-slavery program likely to worsen the crisis. The Fugitive Slave Act of 1850 became the touchstone between Republicans and Democrats, and touching it was a legitimate cause of resistance to the government.

The American Civil War (1861-1865)

Background

In February 1861, shortly after Abraham Lincoln took office, seven states seceded to form a Confederacy, which appointed a government. On April 12, 1861, troops from the army of the Confederate States bomb Fort Sumter near Charleston, South Carolina. This marked the beginning of the Civil War, known as the American Civil War. When Sojourner Truth hears of the Battle of Fort Sumter, she's in Michigan, and although she never wanted war, she supports, without reservation, the Northern troops of the Union Army. Like Frederick Douglass, she sees the conflict as an opportunity to end slavery and for African-Americans to fight for their freedom. This was no longer a time for denouncing slavery, but for supporting the Union and its army.

Southern threats

Shortly afterwards, Sojourner Truth and Josephine Sophia White Griffing, after speaking at a conference organized by Indiana abolitionists, witness riots between southerners and northerners. When they want to speak in

Angola, a mob insults them, threatens them with death, and wants to set fire to the hotel where they are staying. They needed the protection of the Home Guard (Union) to escape the lynching. Both of them criss-cross Steuben County (New York), speaking at women's assemblies to denounce slavery and the (Southern) rebels, and saying they would do so until the end of the war.

Meeting Abraham Lincoln

Despite Abraham Lincoln's diplomatic cautiousness, they reiterated that the war was about slavery and its abolition. When, in April 1862, Congress freed all the slaves residing in the District of Columbia, there was an explosion of joy among abolitionists. Sojourner Truth joined Longwwod's Progressive Friends to present a brief to President Lincoln on the emancipation of slaves, the first meeting between Abraham Lincoln and Sojourner Truth.

Emancipation proclamation in all territories and exactions

On June 18, 1862, Abraham Lincoln signed a declaration abolishing slavery in the territories, and on July 17, 1862, he signed a declaration that became law, freeing all fugitive slaves. Then, with his Secretary of State William Henry Seward and his Secretary of the Treasury Salmon P. Chase, he studied the contents of a proclamation abolishing slavery throughout the United States, to be ready for January 1863. Various military successes against the Confederate armies removed all obstacles. On December 31, 1862, a representative assembly of white and African-American abolitionists was held at the Tremont Temple (en) in Boston. The meeting was chaired by William Cooper Nell (en), and attended by, among others: Frederick Douglass, John Rock (abolitionist) (en) William Lloyd Garrison, Harriet Beecher Stowe, William Wells Brown, Charles Bennett Ray (en). All were aware of the content and date of the presidential proclamation, and prayed for its success. On January 1, 1863, President Abraham Lincoln's Emancipation Proclamation is signed into law. When Sojourner Truth hears the news, she celebrates with her friends "The Glorious Day of Emancipation" and they celebrate "the beginning of the end".

In New York, many residents - mostly Irish-Americans, Southern sympathizers and encouraged by New York governor Horatio Seymour, a Democrat, and New York mayor Fernando Wood - rioted from July 13 to 16, 1863. For these New Yorkers, the Emancipation Proclamation was confirmation that the war was the "Negro's" war, a war in which they did not want to participate. Crowds set fire to the Colored Orphan Asylum, many African-Americans were hanged from lampposts, others were lynched, in a rage to eliminate any African-American presence from New York City. The African-American elite - doctors, pastors, professors, writers - were hunted down; many were lynched, hanged, stoned, burned alive; women were raped. Policemen or soldiers who wanted to protect African-Americans were beaten to death. Governor Horatio Seymour addressed the rioters as "his friends". Isaiah Rynders (en) calls for the destruction of buildings that publish newspapers supporting Abraham Lincoln's policies. The death toll is estimated at 663, but the police count 120, including 106 African-Americans. Sojourner Truth brings help and comfort to the survivors of the massacre.

Support for African-American troops

The Emancipation Proclamation of 1863 opened the doors of the Union Army to African-Americans, who flocked in their thousands. African-American figures such as Frederick Douglass, Charles Lennox Remond, Williams Wells Brown, Martin Delany, Henry McNeal Turner, Josephine St. Pierre Ruffin, Harriet Jacobs and Mary Ann Shadd Cary hold rallies to encourage African-American enlistment.

Frederick Douglass's two sons and one of Martin Delany's sons enlist in the 54th Massachusetts Infantry Regiment, created in the spring of 1863 and commanded by Robert Gould Shaw. The regiment was leased by Sojourner Truth. When he left for the Sea Islands on May 28, 1863, he was joined by an unknown woman, Harriet Tubman, who would later be revealed by the press for her role as a scout and then spy for the Union Army High Command. Newspapers and magazines regularly cited Harriet Tubman and Sojourner Truth as the two most remarkable African-American women.

Sojourner Truth is convinced that enlisting African-Americans is one way to bring the Civil War to a swift end. She immediately embarked on a tour of the Midwest to support the war effort for the Union army.

At the end of 1863, Sojourner Truth, back at her Battle Creek home, appealed to friends and neighbors to provide supplies and food for Union soldiers. She travels to Detroit, offering Thanksgiving dinner to the 102nd United States Colored Infantry Regiment (en) billeted at Camp Ward. Sojourner Truth proudly reiterates her support for the African-American soldiers who enlisted in the Union army.

The re-election of Abraham Lincoln

From September 1864, Sojourner Truth became involved in the campaign for Abraham Lincoln's re-election, notably with her Quaker friends in New Jersey. She then travels to Washington, where she joins Jane Grey Swisshelm, Elizabeth Keckley, the confidante and personal dressmaker of Mary Todd Lincoln, the wife of President

Abraham Lincoln, who runs the *Contraband Relief Association* she founded in 1862. Thanks to Elizabeth Keckley and Lucy N. Colman (en), a meeting is scheduled at the White House between them, Sojourner Truth and President Abraham Lincoln. The meeting takes place at 8 a.m. on October 29, 1864.

This hearing is an opportunity for these two leading figures to recognize and respect each other.

Freedmen's Bureau (1864-1868)

With the Civil War over, Sojourner Truth and her friends Josephine Griffing and Laura Smith Haviland (en) joined the Bureau of Refugees, Freedmen and Abandoned Lands, better known in its abbreviated form as the Freedmen's Bureau. It is a government agency created on the initiative of the late President Lincoln, approved by Congress in 1865 and headed by General Oliver Otis Howard. Its headquarters are in New York. The agency's mission is to assist freed slaves by providing them with daily rations and clothing, medical care, assistance in tracing family members, education through the establishment of schools and Howard University, and the training of African-American teachers. The agency also has full authority to distribute land confiscated from Southerners.

Since Andrew Johnson became president following Abraham Lincoln, appropriations to fund the Freedmen's Bureau have been reduced, and this Democratic president lets the Southern states establish new laws, the Black Codes, which limit the rights of freedmen. It was against this backdrop that Sojourner Truth and her friends joined the Freedmen's Bureau village in Arlington Heights, Virginia, led by Captain George B. Carse. The Bureau has established a hospital that distributes food, clothing and job opportunities to the 250 African-American families under its jurisdiction. But Sojourner Truth noted that malnutrition placed them in a state of dependence that stifled any spirit of initiative, which ran counter to his convictions of the need for African-Americans to emancipate themselves. To support this emancipation, in July 1866 she dictated a letter to her friend Amy Post, who lived in Rochester, to help her organize and carry out her project for voluntary families. In addition, Sojourner Truth, Josephine Griffing and Julia Wilbur (en) lead a campaign against the Village of Arlington, denouncing the attitudes of Bureau executives who deny the aspirations and needs of African-Americans and work only for their salaries. This campaign led to the village's closure in 1868.

Organizing the succession to the Freedmen's Bureau (1867-1868)

Sojourner Truth, Josephine Griffing and Julia Wilbur look for a way to provide jobs for African-Americans in the Refugee Bureau village of Arlington Heights. Starting in the spring of 1867, they sent them to more employable states such as Michigan and New York. Sojourner Truth returned to her home in Battle Creek, Michigan, where she managed to provide employment for around a hundred refugees. For her part, Josephine Griffing managed to place between three and five hundred refugees between 1866 and 1868. With the combined efforts of the Freedmen's Bureau and the initiatives of Sojourner Truth, Josephine Griffing, Julia Wilbur and others, over 8,000 refugees were hired in the Battle Creek, Brockport, Rochester and Providence areas... These good figures are not satisfactory, however, because for the operations to be successful, employers would have to agree to hire all members of the same family of working age in the same location, but the men were sent to farms and the women were employed as domestic servants. Very few employ the elderly, leaving them in poverty. This fragmentation of families affects their morale.

Women's right to vote

In 1866, Sojourner Truth joined the Women's Loyal National League (en) founded in 1863 by Susan B. Anthony and Elizabeth Cady Stanton. Anthony and Elizabeth Cady Stanton. The organization's primary mission was to financially support the Union Army's war efforts during the American Civil War and the Thirteenth Amendment to the U.S. Constitution. After the war, the Women's Loyal National League turned its attention to the defense of women's rights, and in particular to obtaining the right to vote for women. Sojourner Truth feels isolated as an African-American woman defending the rights of black women. Susan B. Anthony sent her a letter in January 1866, informing her that she was going to add her name to a petition drafted by herself, Elizabeth Cady Stanton and Lucy Stone and addressed to the members of Congress who had created the Women's Rights Commission.

In 1867, Sojourner Truth spoke at the American Equal Rights Association convention, where she drew attention to the plight of recently freed women of color, reiterating the link between white and black women's rights.

This movement by abolitionists towards women's rights after the Civil War is also shared by African-American figures such as Frederick Douglass, Josephine Griffing, Charles Lenox Remond, Robert Purvis and others. It's a movement where blacks and whites come together. Women's rights impacted on their wages, inheritance rights, child custody, access to university education and career choices.

Land reserved for African-Americans in America or Liberia?

The controversial colonization of Liberia

In 1870, noting the state of exclusion and poverty of the freedmen, Sojourner Truth had an article published in the *New York Tribune* in which she stated that she was dedicated to finding land for African-Americans, where they would find the means to live by themselves and for themselves - indicating that there was ample land available in the American West beyond the Mississippi. If there are reservations for Native Americans, wouldn't it be possible to do the same for freedmen and thus solve the refugee question and the cost of financing refugee camps? Sojouner Truth's proposal is linked to her belief in the empowerment of African-Americans by freeing them from their dependence on government handouts. A solution she found simpler than transplantation to Sierra Leone or colonization of Liberia, proposed by Paul Cuffe in 1815 and the American Colonization Society (ACS) in 1816. This project, quickly criticized by leaders of the African-American community (Richard Allen, Absalom Jones, James Forten), was nevertheless revived after the Civil War by Henry McNeal Turner and others, who saw in it an opportunity for African-Americans to live free with civil rights. This idea was rejected by Sojourner Truth.

A context of violence

His concern also arises against the backdrop of rising violence on the part of the Ku Klux Klan and other supremacist organizations sowing terror among African-Americans. This observation was shared by Henry Adams and Benjamin "Pap" Singleton, both of whom joined Sojourner Truth in his petition to Congress to find unoccupied territories in America to be colonized by African-Americans. This petition was also supported by his Boston friend, the Reverend Gilbert Haven (en). In March 1870, Sojourner Truth traveled to Washington, where she met with President Ulysses S. Grant and several Republican senators like Charles Charles. Grant and several Republican senators, including Charles Sumner, Henry Wilson, George Washington Julian (en) and black senator Hiram Rhodes Revels, to promote her project. On January 1, 1871, Sojourner Truth spoke at a meeting held at Boston's Tremont Temple (en) to celebrate the eighth anniversary of the Emancipation Proclamation, where she presented her proposal. The meeting was organized by the American Temperance Society, representatives of the Freedmen's Schools (en) and chaired by William Wells Brown.

The project to set up in the American West

During her speech, Sojourner Truth forcefully repeated her idea of settling African-Americans in available territories in the American West beyond the Mississippi, rather than leaving them parked in camps run by the Freedmen's Bureau, and asked for support for her petition. In February 1871, the Reverend Gilbert Haven published her petition in the columns of his newspaper *Zion's Herald*, now *The Progressive Christian (en)*, published in Boston. Its success led Horace Greeley to publish the petition in the *New York Tribune* in March 1871, and finally in the *National Anti-Slavery Standard*.

In June 1871, Sojourner Truth returned to Battle Creek to notarize the purchase of her College Avenue home and pay off her mortgage. Once this was done, she headed for Detroit to continue supporting her project to establish a presence in the American West. During her visit, the Detroit *Daily Post* praises her commitment to both the abolition of slavery and women's rights, and attaches her petition to the report of her conference. She also receives the support of Reverend Charles C. Foote (en), Detroit's prison chaplain, who collects the signed petitions and sends them to Washington.

Locating territories in Kansas

In a letter dated December 31, 1870, Byron M. Smith of Topeka, Kansas, invited Sojourner Truth to travel there, all expenses paid, to present settlement possibilities. In September 1871, Sojourner Truth took the train to fulfill his invitation, and the two of them traveled throughout Kansas for five months. She gave regular lectures on settlement, women's rights and the fight against alcoholism, repeating that women's suffrage would put an end to the flawed governance and corruption that undermined political life. The results of this tour were disappointing. Neither Sojourner Truth nor Byron M. Smith were able to establish any concrete basis for settlements, probably due to a lack of buyers with the necessary funds. In the end, the project remained as vague as it had been in 1871.

The return to Battle Creek, the abandonment of the American project

Sojourner Truth and her friends continue to collect signatures for her petition. To this end, she crisscrosses Michigan, holding conferences in Detroit, Grand Rapids, Kalamazoo, Saginaw, Ann Harbor and Adrian, while at the same time campaigning in support of her presidential candidate, Ulysses S. Grant. Grant was re-elected, allowing her to rest during the winter of 1872-1873. In the spring of 1873, she resumed her work on behalf of the settlements, and at the same time helped the people of Detroit and Grand Rapids to found a local chapter of the Woman's Christian Temperance Union and a chapter of the Order of the Eastern Star. After three years of campaigning for her settlement project, she travels to Washington and, with the support of her friend General Oliver Otis Howard, dictates a letter to both Benjamin Franklin Butler, a member of the House of Representatives, and a Civil War general, requesting funding for her project. Benjamin Butler in turn sent a letter to Charles Sumner, a member of the Senate. Despite the joint efforts of Sojourner Truth and Benjamin Butler, the project was never presented to Congress. It was finally abandoned by Sojourner Truth in the spring of 1874.

Illness and the end of his career

At the end of 1874, Sojourner Truth fell ill, a hemiplegia paralyzing her entire right side, and leg ulcers developed that would never go away. On her doctor's orders, she was confined to bed for two months, and seeing her condition, her friend Dr. John Harvey Kellogg had her admitted to his sanatorium in Battle Creek, where the health staff gave her the best possible care. Despite her illness, she resumed her lecture series from 1878 to 1880. These were transcribed and published in the press, notably by *The Christian Recorder (en)* of Philadelphia, organ of the African Methodist Episcopal Church, *The Woman's Tribune (en)* linked to the American Woman Suffrage Association, the *Chicago Inter Ocean...* In 1880, although she could no longer move about, people visited her at her Battle Creek home, where she was cared for by her daughters until her death in 1883. Right up to her last moments, she was playful with visitors, especially journalists, and never lost her sense of humor.

Privacy policy

Sojourner Truth died of exhaustion at her last home, Battle Creek, on November 26, 1883, her last words being "follow the teaching of our Lord Jesus". She is buried in *Oak Hill* Cemetery in Battle Creek.

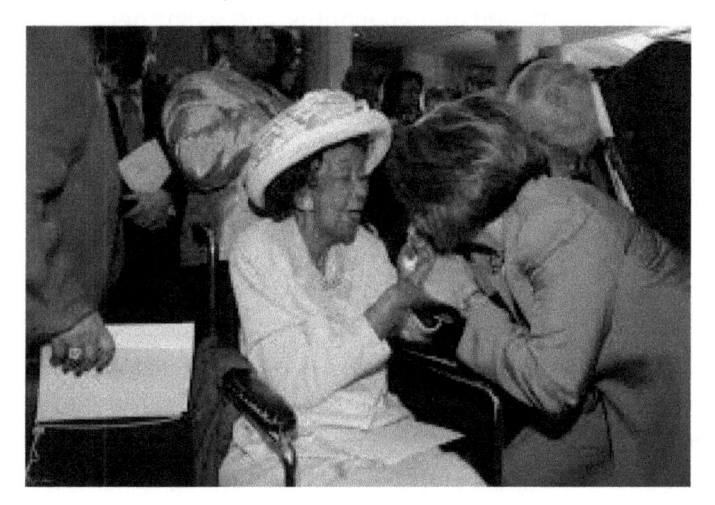

Written transcriptions by Sojourner Truth

The following works are critical reference editions, without prejudice to other editions.

Bilingual English-French version

- Sojourner Truth (trans. Françoise Bouillot, pref. Pap Ndiaye), *Et ne suis-je pas une femme? = And ain't I a woman?* (speech), Paris, Payot, 2021, 141 p. (ISBN 9782228928632, read online)

In American

- (en-US) Gilbert Olive & Frances W. Titus (eds.), *Narrative of Sojourner Truth*, Salem, New Hampshire, Ayer Company Publisher / Beaufort Books (repr. 1878, 1974,) (1 ed. 1850), 320 p. (ISBN 9780405018411, OCLC 1036786904, read online), Lydia Maria Child,

- (en-US) Patricia C. McKissack & Fredrick L. McKissack (eds.), *Sojourner Truth: Ain't I a Woman?*, New York, Scholastic, November 1, 1992, 200 p. (ISBN 9780590446907, read online),

- (en-US) Suzanne Pullon Fitch (ed.), *Sojourner Truth as Orator: Wit, Story, and Song*, Westport, Connecticut, Greenwood Press, September 23, 1997, 272 p. (ISBN 9780313300684, read online),

Archives

The Sojourner Truth archives are deposited and available for consultation at the "Sojourner Truth" Library of the State University of New York at New Paltz.

> 48 NARRATIVE OF
>
> indeed sitting, and again commenced to relate her injuries. After holding some conversation among themselves, one of them rose, and bidding her follow him, led the way to a side office, where he heard her story, and asked her 'if she could *swear* that the child she spoke of was her son?' 'Yes,' she answered, 'I *swear* it's my son.' 'Stop, stop!' said the lawyer, 'you must swear by this book'—giving her a book, which she thinks must have been the Bible. She took it, and putting it to her lips, began again to swear it was her child. The clerks, unable to preserve their gravity any longer, burst into an uproarious laugh; and one of them inquired of lawyer Chip of what use it could be to make *her* swear. 'It will answer the law,' replied the officer. He then made her comprehend just what he wished her to do, and she took a lawful oath, as far as the outward ceremony could make it one. All can judge how far she understood its spirit and meaning.
>
> He now gave her a writ, directing her to take it to the constable of New Paltz, and have him serve it on Solomon Gedney. She obeyed, walking, or rather *trotting*, in her haste, some eight or nine miles.
>
> But while the constable, through mistake, served the writ on a brother of the real culprit, Solomon Gedney slipped into a boat, and was nearly across the North River, on whose banks they were standing, before the dull Dutch constable was aware of his mistake. Solomon Gedney, meanwhile, consulted a lawyer, who advised him to go to Alabama and bring back the boy, otherwise it might cost him fourteen years' imprisonment, and a thousand dollars in cash. By this time, it is hoped he began to feel that selling slaves unlawfully was not so good a business as he had wished to find it. He secreted himself till due preparations could be made, and soon set

Tributes

- In 1971, the State University of New York at New Paltz named its new library "Sojourner Truth",

- In 1986, Sojourner Truth was inducted into the National Women's Hall of Fame.

- Sojourner Truth is one of 39 guests seated in the installation *The Dinner Party* (1974-1979) by feminist artist Judy Chicago.

- 1983: Induction ceremony into the Michigan Women's Hall of Fame.

- In 1986, illustrator Jerry Pinkney drew a portrait of Sojourner Truth for the United States Postal Service, which served as the effigy for a 22-cent stamp issued on February 4, 1986.

- African-American artist Faith Ringgold pays tribute to him in her painting *The Sunflowers Quilting Bee at Arles*.

- In 1997, the robot of the *Mars Pathfinder* space probe - a NASA mission to explore the planet Mars - was named "Sojourner", in his memory.

- In 2002, a statue of Sojourner Truth was erected in Florence, a village near Northampton, Massachusetts, in memory of his arrival in 1843.

- In 2006, President George W. Bush signed a bill authorizing the permanent display of a Bust of Sojourner Truth (U.S. Capitol) in the Emancipation Hall of the U.S. Capitol Visitor Center, created by sculptor Artis Lane and inaugurated on April 28, 2009.

- In 2014, *Smithsonian* (magazine) named Sojourner Truth to its list of the 100 most important Americans of all time.

- In 2020, Andrew M. Cuomo, Governor of New York State, unveiled a statue of Sojourner Truth in the State Historic Park near the Hudson River Bridge in Ulster County to celebrate the centenary of women's suffrage in the United States.

- In astronomy, Truth, an asteroid in the main asteroid belt, and Truth, a crater on the planet Venus, are also named in his honor (249521).

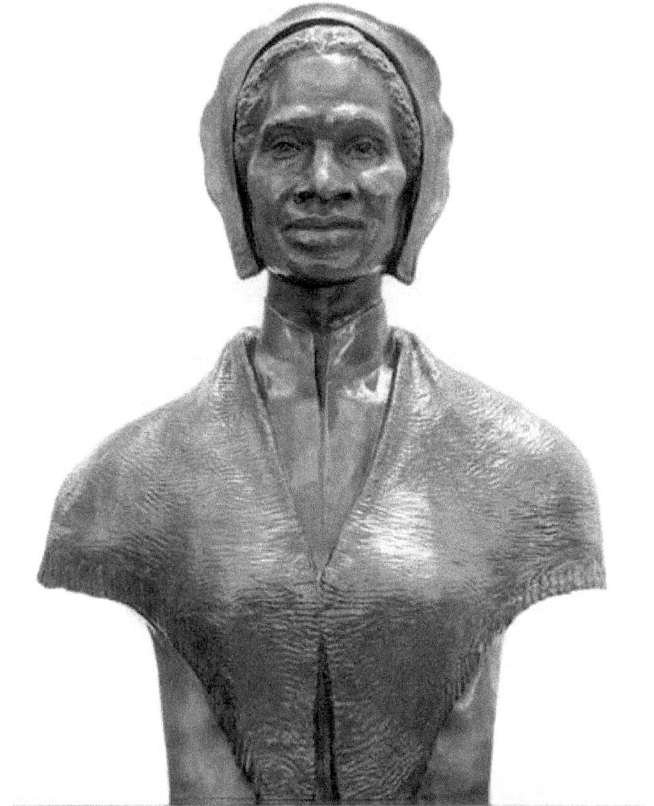

Other books by United Library

https://campsite.bio/unitedlibrary

Milton Keynes UK
Ingram Content Group UK Ltd.
UKHW050200130724
445574UK00014B/715